ROUND PEAK CLAWHAMMER
BANJO
Traditional Appalachian Fiddle Tunes from Surry County, NC

by Joseph Weidlich

ISBN 978-1-57424-409-0
SAN 683-8022

Cover Banjo made by Kyle Creed

Cover by James Creative Group

Copyright © 2022 CENTERSTREAM Publishing
P.O. Box 17878 - Anaheim Hills, CA 92817

www.centerstream-usa.com | centerstrm@aol.com | 714-779-9390

TABLE OF CONTENTS

INTRODUCTION

The Round Peak area of Surry County, North Carolina consists of a number of small communities which border Mt. Airy, NC. The Round Peak musical style is synonymous with the old time music pairing of the fiddle with the African-derived banjo and was considered to be the defining ensemble sound for community dance music.

It is clear that earlier generations of Round Peak fiddle and banjo players added techniques to their own playing which they learned directly from African-American musicians whom had travelled through or lived in the area for decades. In short, their performance style became "rougher" than the players on the "backside of the mountain" in nearby Galax, VA, by (1) incorporating African-American syncopations and driving rhythms into their playing; (2) by varying the structure of songs by stripping them down or by adding new parts to create new songs (for example, Step Back Cindy, Sally Ann, John Brown's Dream, etc.); and (3) by playing extra reiterations of the lower strain of dance tunes (referred to as the "coarse" part by fiddlers) instead of adhering to the traditional AA BB format.

As most of the Round Peak repertoire is played in the traditional keys of either D Major or A Major those are the keys that I have used in the following arrangements (indicated by D or A in the brackets following each song title in the Song List).

NOTES ON THE ARRANGEMENTS

Hammer-Ons and Pull-Offs. The notations used in the tablatures for this collection are, for the most part, straight forward. For instance, hammer-ons and pull-offs are notated by the use of slurs; there is even an open string hammer-on used in *Lost Indian* on the fourth string.

Slides. The first note of slide figures are clearly articulated; however, there is no definite ending point depending on which left hand finger is used to execute the slide, particularly as Round Peak banjo players prefer to use fretless banjos. Thus I decided not to use slur marks for notating slides. In my playing, after I play the initial note, I gradually release the finger pressure as I play the slide to simulate the sound of a fretless slide; however, 2-4 or 2-5 slides can also be played with a definite ending point.

Open String Pull-Offs. Open string pull-offs were first documented in the earliest published banjo instructors by Tom Briggs in his *Banjo Instructor* (1855) and Phil Rice in his *Correct Method for the Banjo* (1858). While Briggs preferred to use a glide stroke to play the open string followed by a hammer-on Rice used a left hand finger to pluck the open string followed by a drop thumb movement, which is how it is normally played in contemporary usage. Here is an example of that period usage:

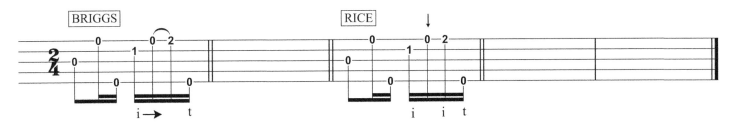

Phil Rice also used this technique to play the second string open. Here is a short banjo break (called a *Symphony* in the parlance of the day) from the song *Do, Mr. Boker, Do* which demonstrates this usage:

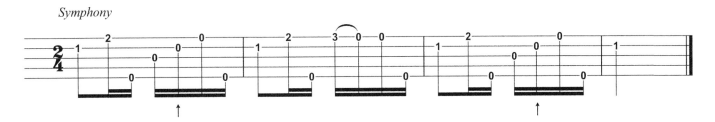

In the tunes in this collection this type of open string pull-off is usually confined to the first string; however, in the fiddle tune *Old Molly Hare* it is also used on the second string.

Alternating Thumb Stroke. One principal characteristic of Round Peak banjoist Kyle Creed's playing style was his frequent use of playing the fifth string on most of the weak beats. Again, this was a common technique used by the first generation of minstrel banjoists. Let's look at opening of Briggs' arrangement of *Old Joe*:

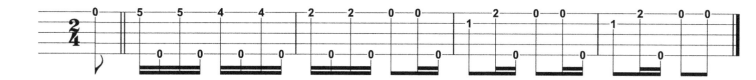

Here is a slightly more involved example from the tune *Briggs' Reel*:

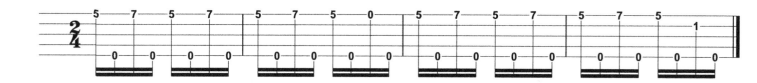

Next is an even more complex example used by Briggs to begin the B section of his arrangement of *Darkey Fishers Hornpipe* (note the "melodic style" of playing in the final measure by using the fifth string as a melodic note):

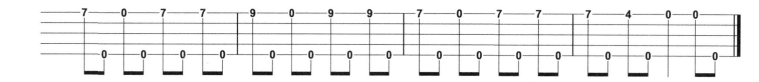

Round Peak banjo players often incorporate playing some type of articulated note when playing the fifth string on the weak beat, usually when playing slides; however, I decided not to notate that type of usage in my tabs to avoid unnecessary clutter. Here is an example using that type of figure with a pull-off:

Drop Thumb Technique. Interestingly, while Briggs frequently used the standard drop thumb technique (first string-second string-first string-thumb string) Rice does not (no o most of the Round Peak banjo players!). In fact, Rice used what he called a *"Double Strike"* stroke sequence which is the reverse note sequence: first string-thumb string-first string-second string. Fred Cockerham often used this technique in his playing (as did Briggs).

Brush Stokes. Round Peak banjo players prefer to minimize the use of the chordal style brush strokes except for certain accented melodic effects. One exception is the Galax Lick. Kyle Creed referred to this type of brush stroke as "raking" the strings. This roll was first documented in Briggs *Banjo Instructor* in the song *Wait for the Wagon*. Here is the opening section:

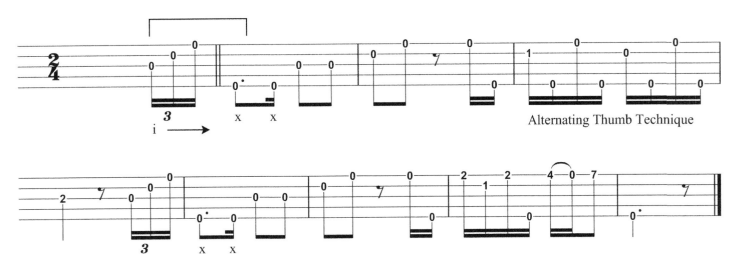

Briggs used this type of right hand fingering in several other songs which led to the Galax Lick rhythmic figure. Here is an example:

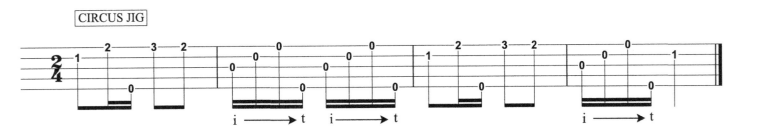

As you can see, if the rhythm in measure two is slightly varied you easily end up with a Galax style lick. In fact, this particular lick is identical to the note sequence I showed earlier in the *symphony* for the minstrel song *Do, Mr. Boker, Do* where Phil Rice used an open string pull off <u>instead</u> of the glide stroke used by Tom Briggs in this example.

Index-Thumb Fingerings. When quarter notes are used in succession on adjacent strings I used the index finger to play the note on the higher string followed by the thumb on the following adjacent lower string (see the B section of *Big Eyed Rabbit* for such an example). This was a commonly used right hand technique documented in the earliest banjo methods.

Big Eyed Rabbit

Open A Tuning

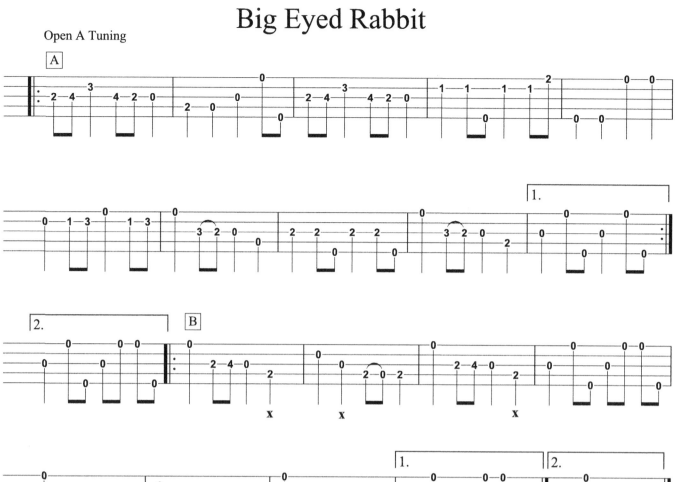

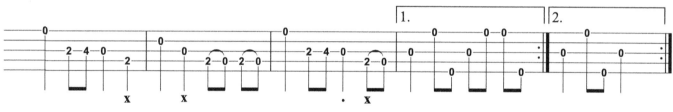

Caption

Big Liza No. 1

Double D Tuning

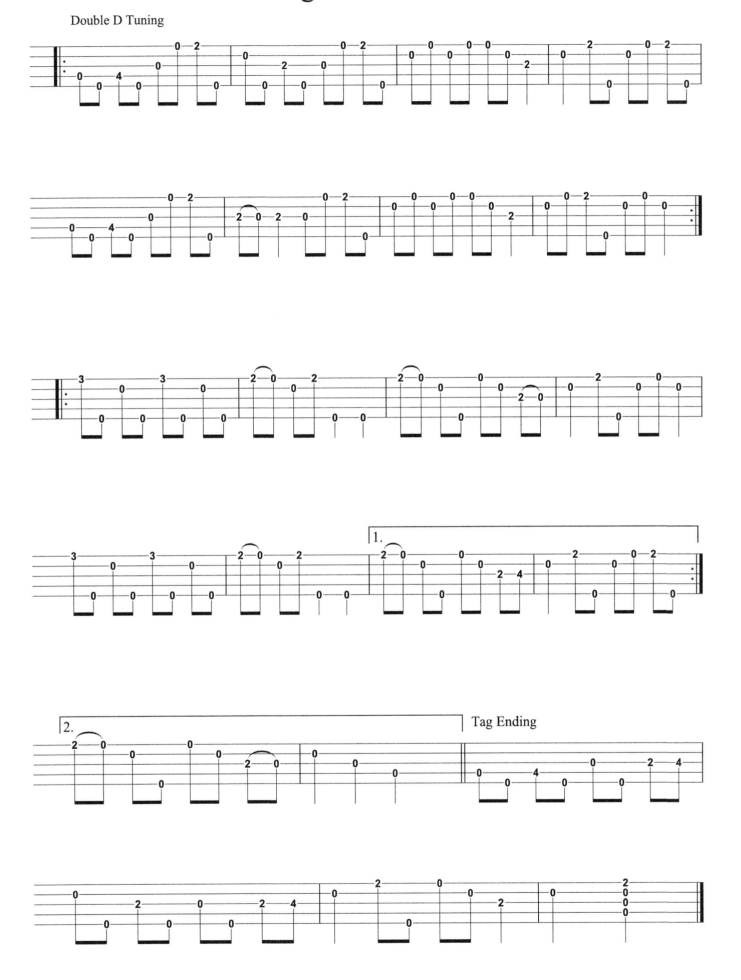

Big Liza No. 2

Double D Tuning

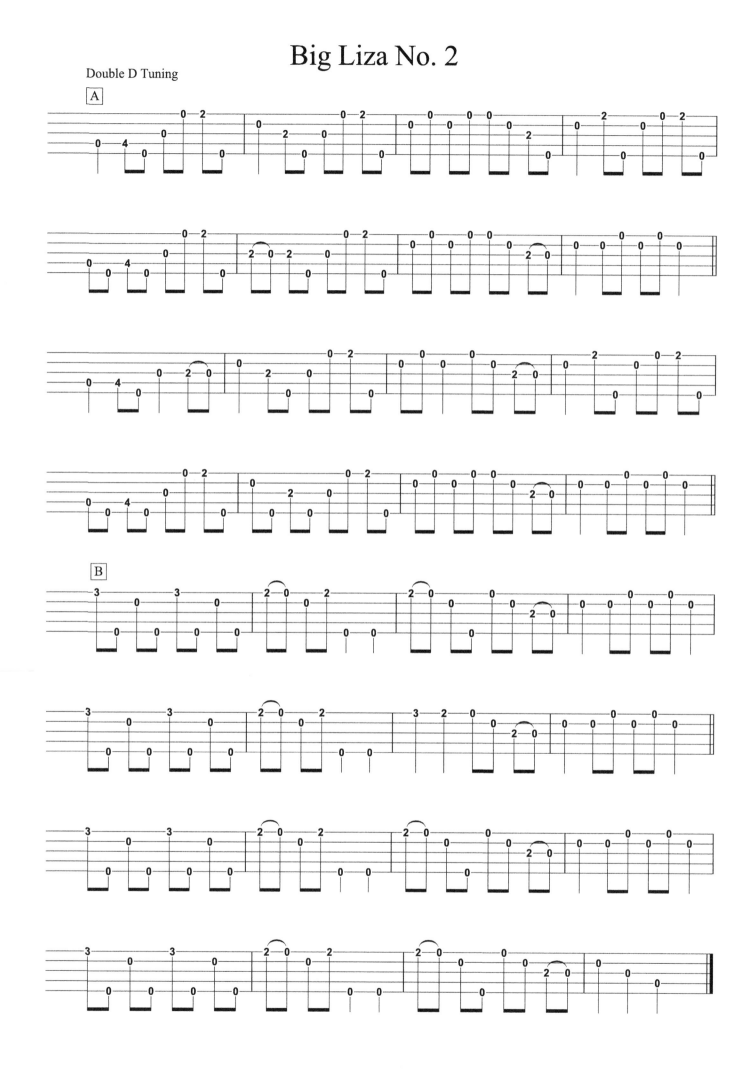

Black Eyed Susie

Double D Tuning

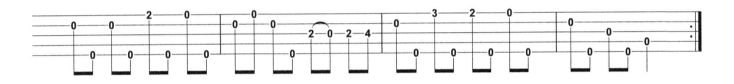

Breaking Up Christmas

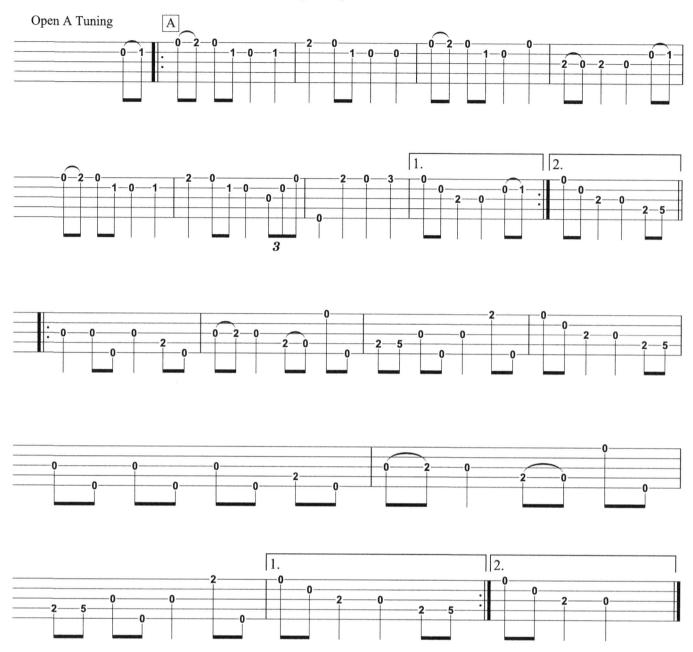

Cluck Old Hen

Open A Tuning

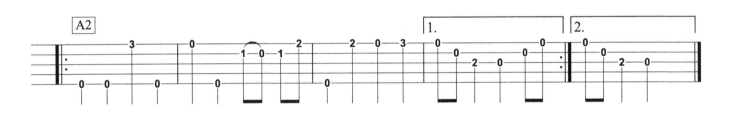

The Camp Creed Boys are (back, L-R): Fred Cockerhan, Kyle Creed, Emos East (Front L-R):,Paul Sutphin, Vertin Cliftin, Ronald Collins

Ducks on the Millpond

Double D Tuning

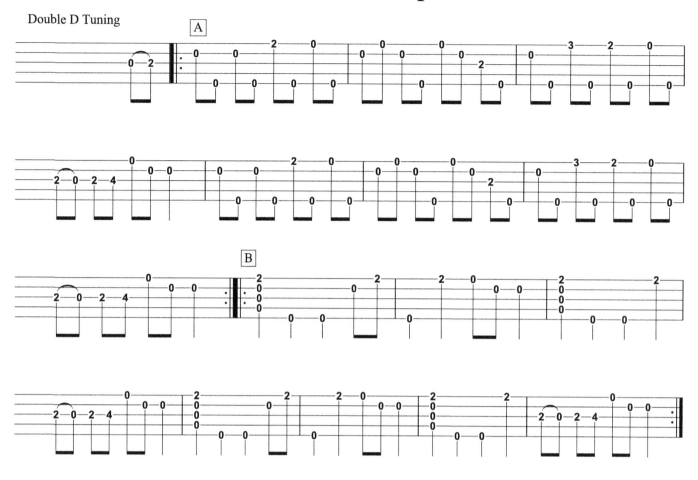

Kyle Creed

Fortune

Double D Tuning

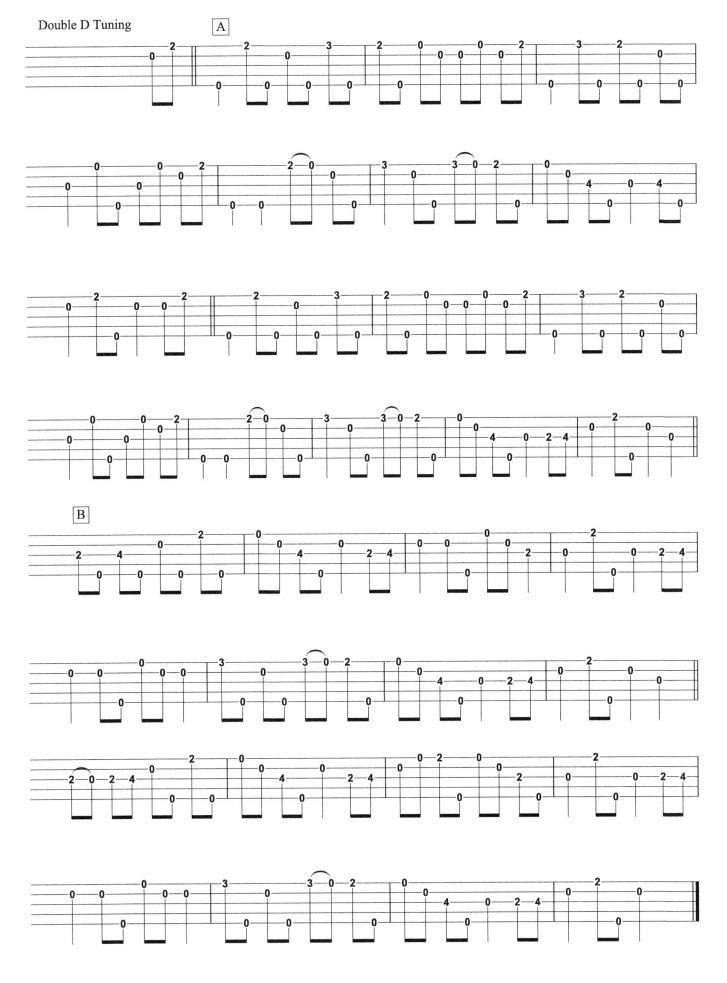

John Brown's Dream

Open A Tuning

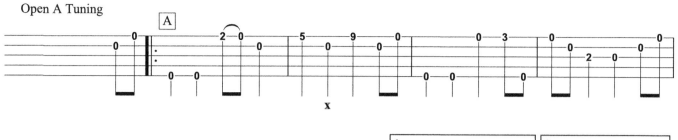

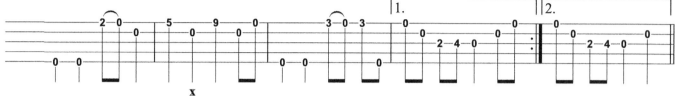

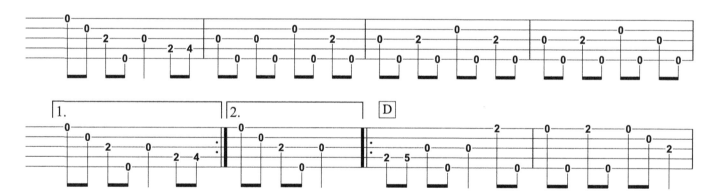

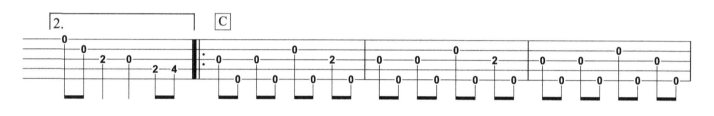

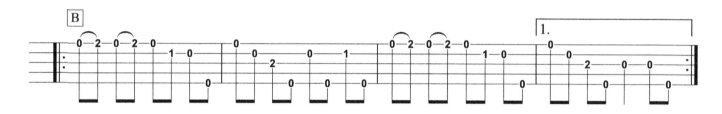

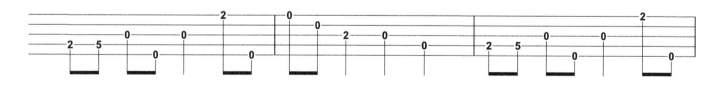

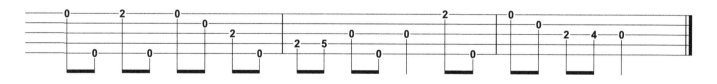

John Hardy

Open A Tuning

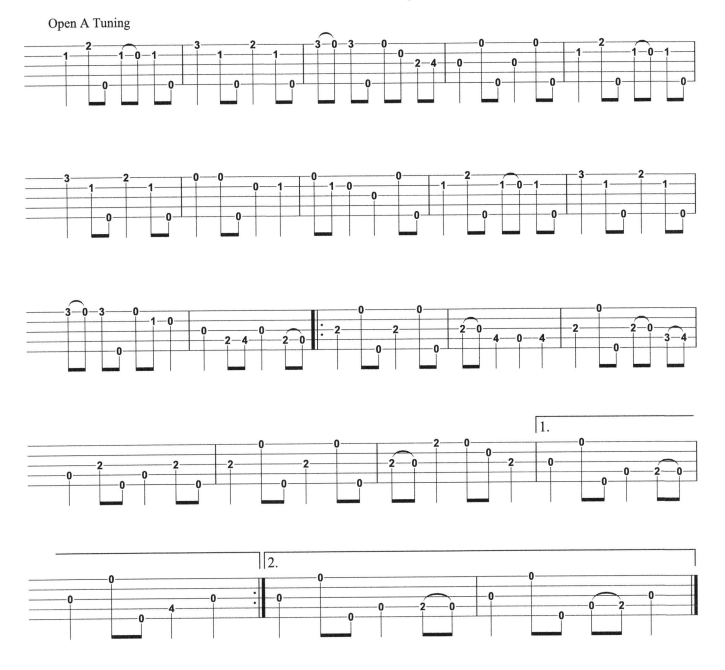

John Henry

Open A Tuning

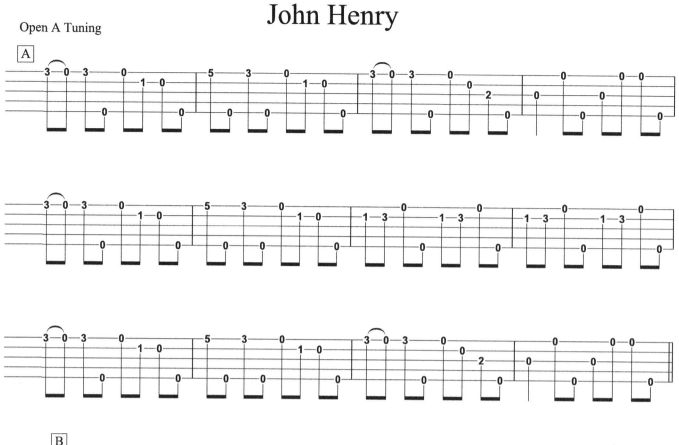

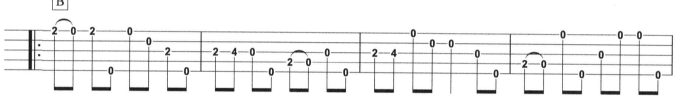

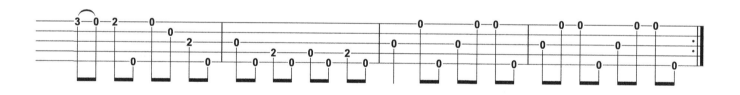

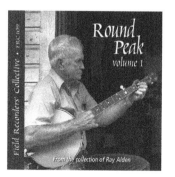

18

Katy Kline

Double D Tuning

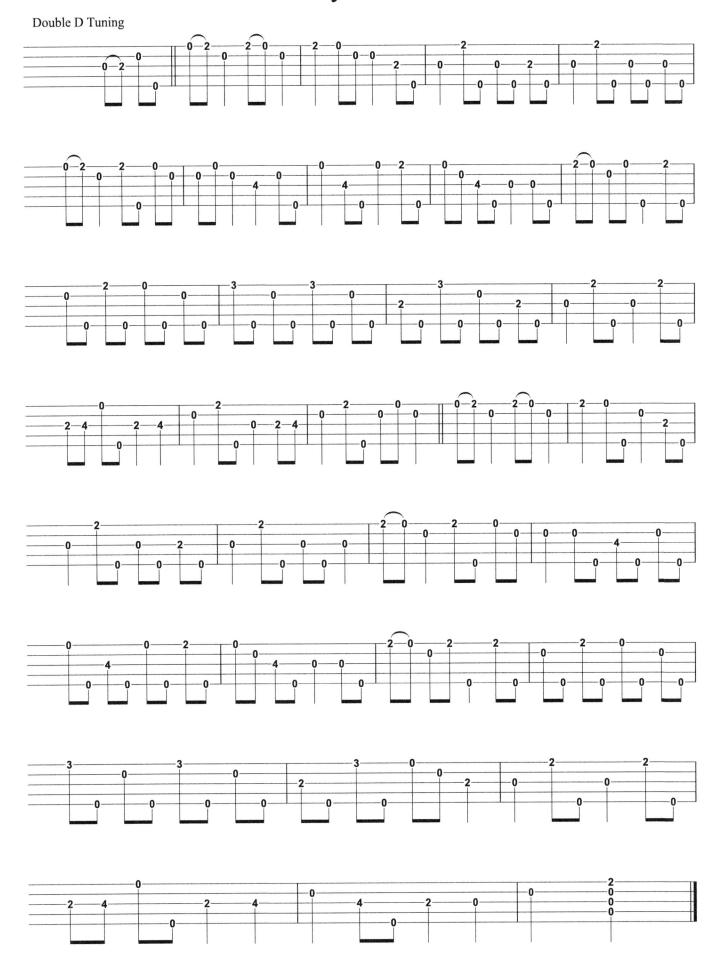

Let Me Fall

Open A Tuning

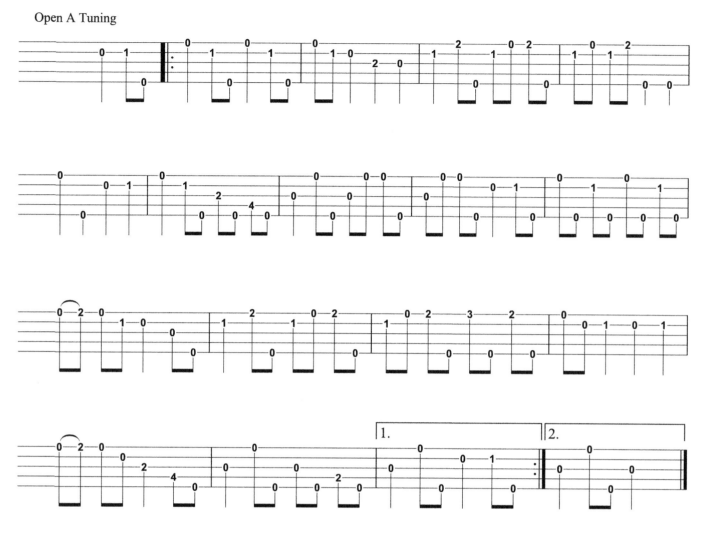

Advertisment for Kyle Creed Banjos

Little Liza Jane

Double D Tuning

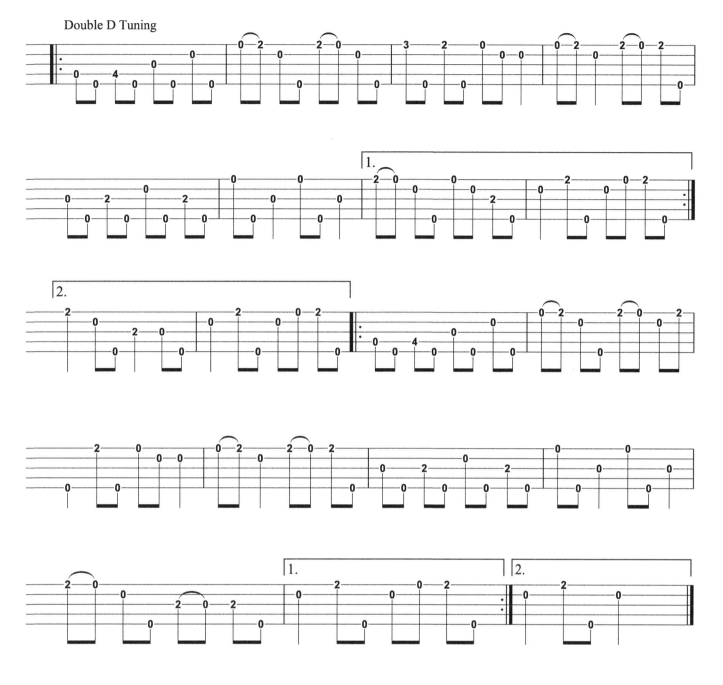

Lost Indian

Open A Tuning

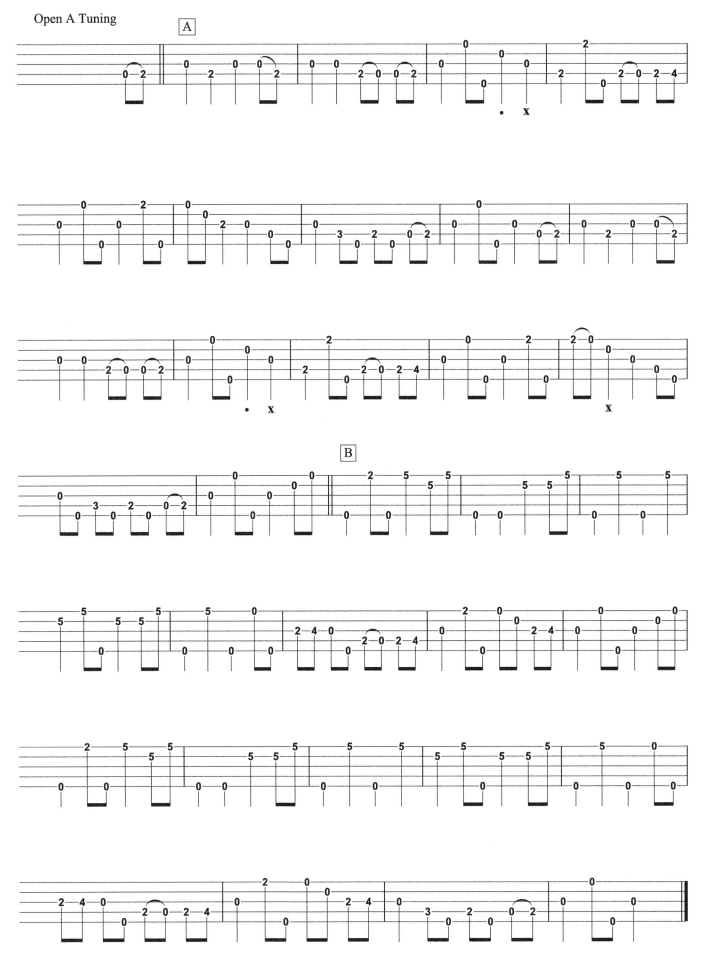

Old Joe Clark

Open A Tuning

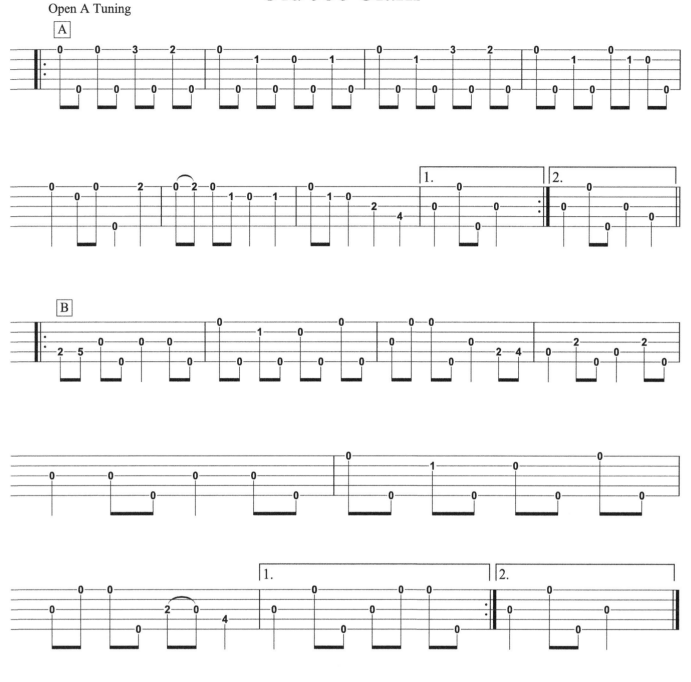

Old Molly Hare

Double D Tuning

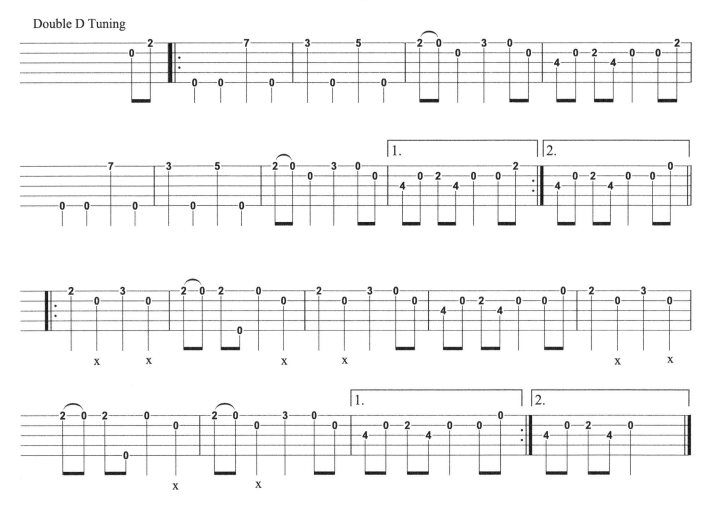

Polly Put the Kettle On

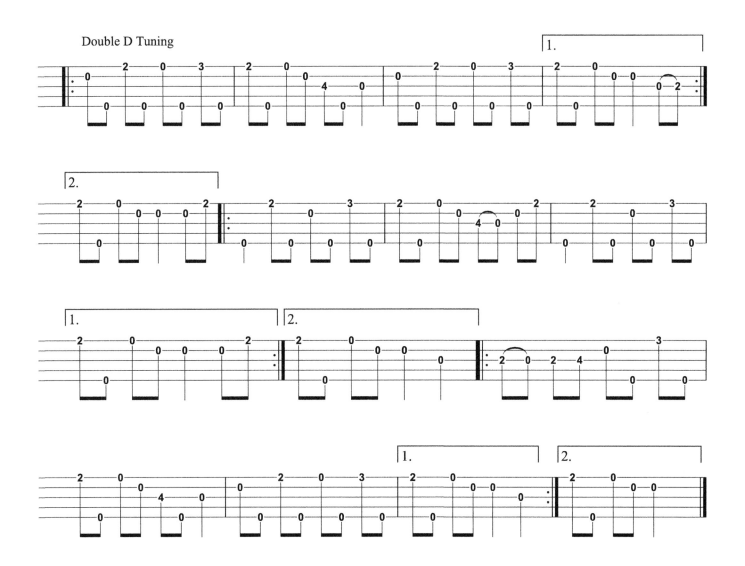

Pretty Little Girl

Open A Tuning

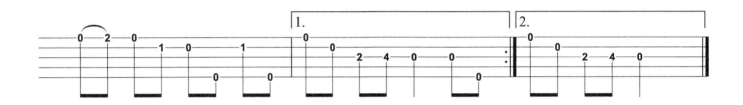

Rockingham Cindy

Double D Tuning

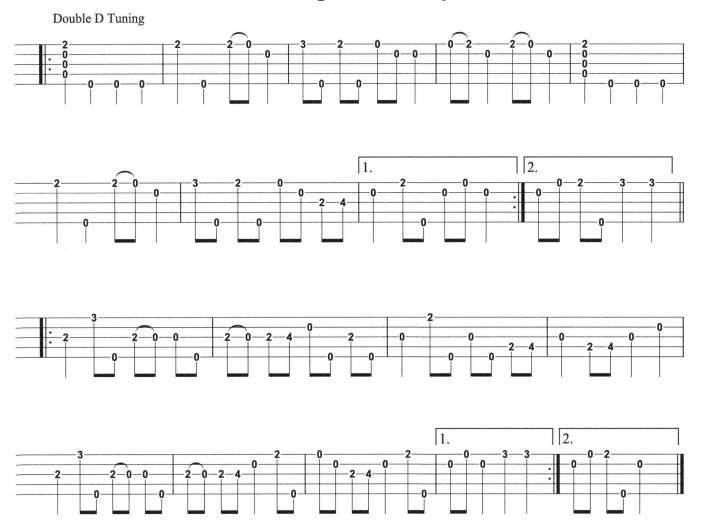

Roustabout

Double D Tuning

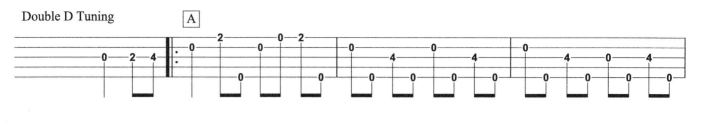

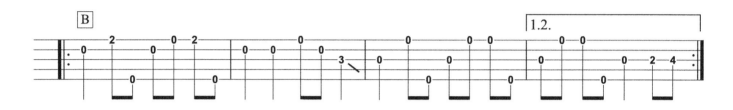

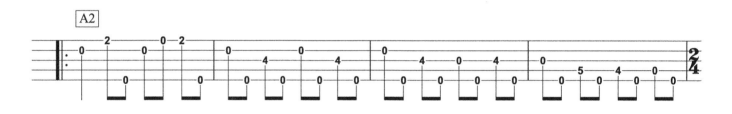

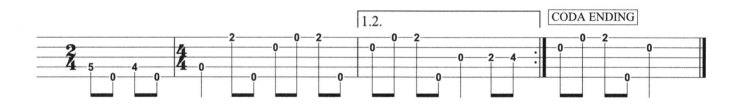

Sail Away Ladies

Open A Tuning

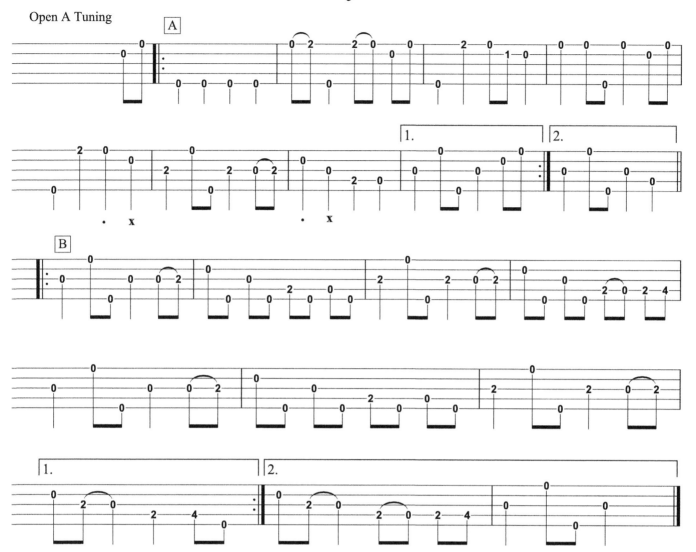

Sally Ann

Double D tuning

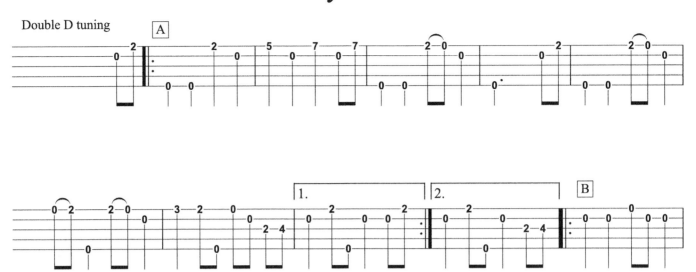

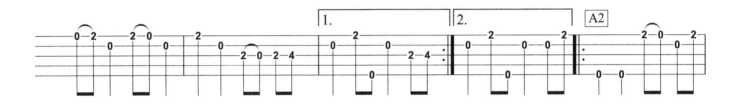

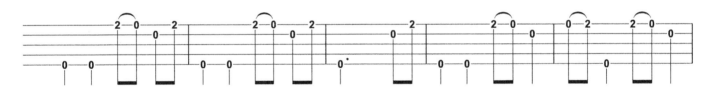

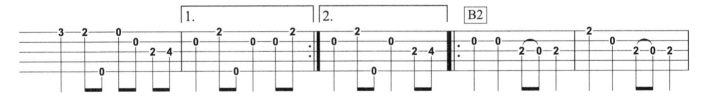

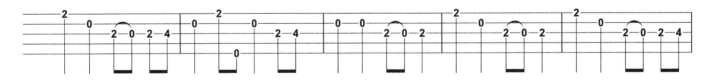

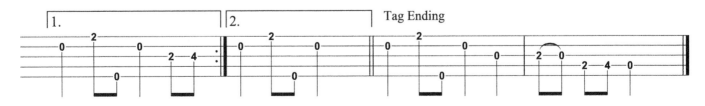

Step Back Cindy

Double D Tuning

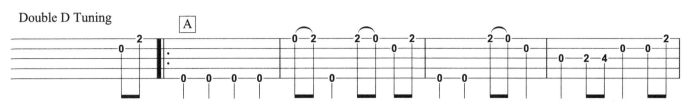

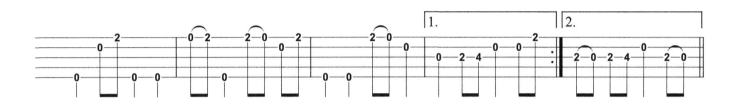

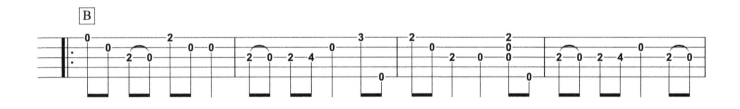

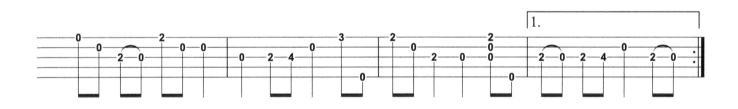

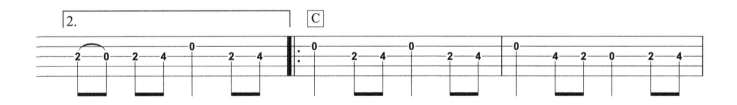

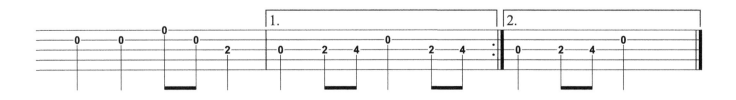

Stillhouse

Double D Tuning

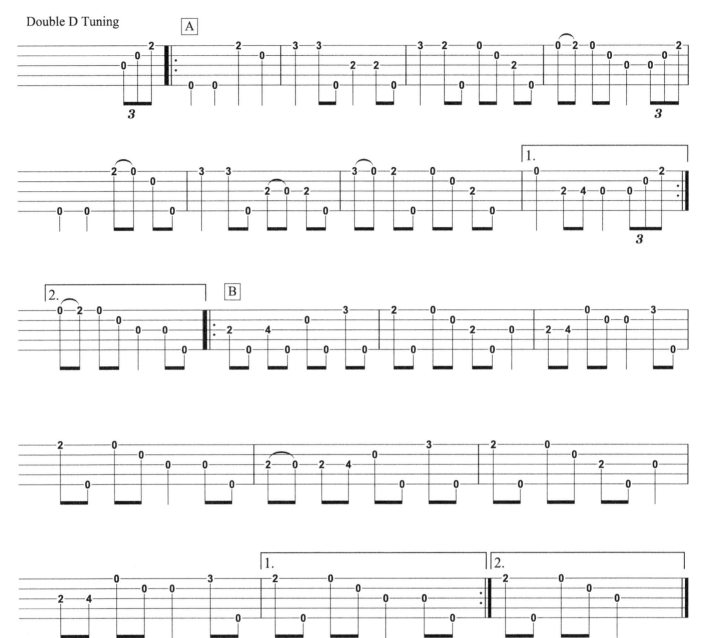

Sugar Hill

Double D Tuning

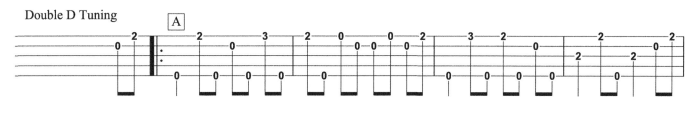

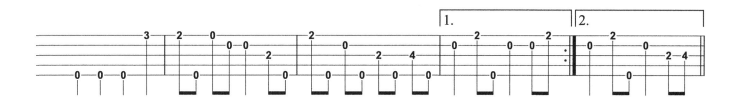

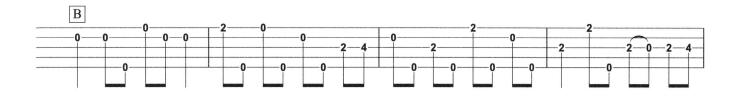

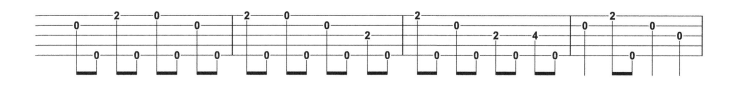

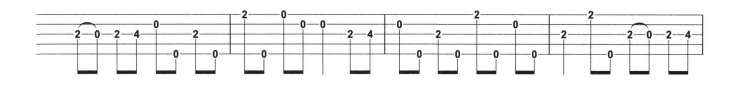

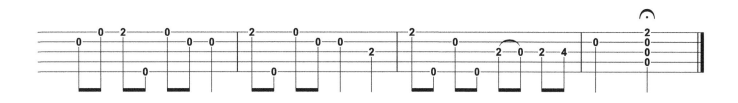

Susanna Gal

Double D Tuning

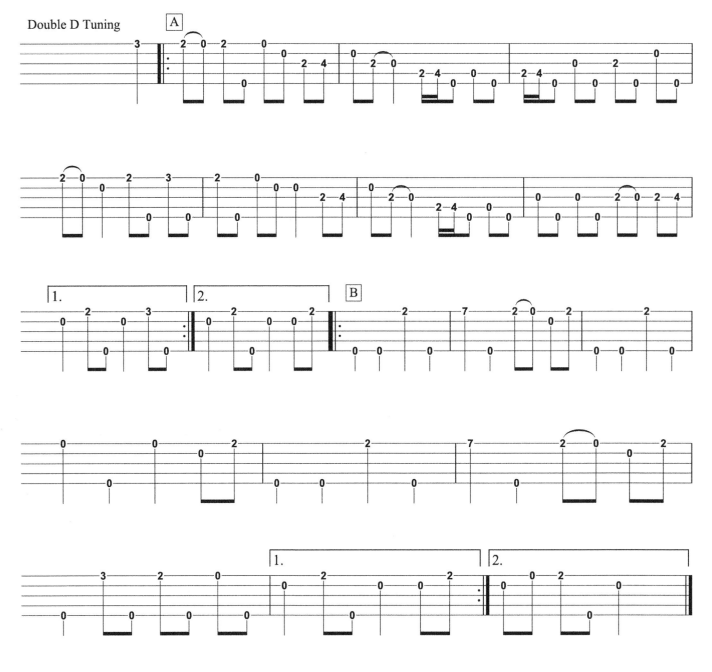

RELATED REFERENCE MATERIALS

American Antebellum Fiddling
Chris Goertzen
University Press of Mississippi – Jackson (2020)

Appalachian Fiddle Music
Drew Beisswenger and Roy Andrade (with Scott Prouty)
Mel Bay Publications, Inc. (2021)

George P. Knauff's Virginia Reels and the History of American Fiddling
Chris Goertzen
University Press of Mississippi – Jackson (2017)

Hoedowns, Reels, and Frolics:
Roots and Branches of Southern Appalachian Dance
Phi Jamison
University of Illinois Press (2015)

Images of America: Surry County, North Carolina
Surry County Genealogical Association
See Chapter 10, Stewart's Creek Township for information on the Round Peak communities.

Making Round Peak Music: History, Revitalization and Community
PhD dissertation by James Randolph Ruchala (May 2011)

Minstrel Banjo: Briggs' Banjo Instructor
Performance Notes and Transcriptions by Joseph Weidlich
Centerstream Publishing (1997)

The Creolization of American Culture:
William Sydney Mount and the Roots of Blackface Minstrelsy
Christopher J. Smith
University of Illinois Press (2013)

ROUND PEAK SELECT DISCOGRAPHY

Camp Creek Boys (County Records CD-2719)

Clawhammer Banjo Volume One [County Records CD 2716]

Clawhammer Banjo Volume Two [County Records CD 2717]

Clawhammer Banjo Volume Three [County Records CD 2718]

Down to the Cider Mill (County Records 2734)

Fred Cockerham (Field Recorder's Collective FRC-101)

June Apple (Heritage Records HRC-CD-038)

Kyle Creed & His Clawhammer Banjo: Liberty [Heritage Records HRC-CD-028]

Round Peak Volume 1 (Field Recorder's Collective FRC-109)

Round Peak Volume 2 (Field Recorder's Collective FRC-110)

Stay All Night (County Records CD 2735)

Tommy Jarrell Volume 1 (County Records 2724)

Tommy Jarrell Volume 2 (County Records 2725)

Tommy Jarrell Volume 3 (County Records 2726)

Tommy Jarrell Volume 4 (County Records 2727)

Tommy & Fred (County Records CD-2702)

More Great Banjo Books from Centerstream...

400 SMOKIN' BLUEGRASS BANJO LICKS

by Eddie Collins

Know only 20 solo licks? How about 50? 100? 200? If that's all, then you need this book, designed to help you improvise bluegrass style solos. 400 licks are played over standard chord progressions; the use of licks sometimes will take precedent over stating the melody. The progressions used are based primarily on common vocal numbers. Some of the licks included are: chromatic licks, embellishing a fiddletune, high position licks, Reno style, pentatonic blues, boogie licks, swing phrasing, sequential licks, back-up licks and many more. Uses standard G tuning. Companion book: 400 Smokin Bluegrass Guitar Licks (#00123172).
00123175 Book/CD Pack..$19.99

GIBSON MASTERTONE
Flathead 5-String Banjos of the 1930's and 1940's
by Jim Mills

While Gibson produced literally thousands of banjos prior to WWII, only 250 or so featured that "Magic Combination" of an Original Flathead Tonering and Five-string neck. 19 of the absolute best are featured here. With details of their known histories and provenances, as well as never-before-seen photos, bills of sale, factory shipping ledgers, and other ephemera relating to these rare and highly desirable instruments..
00001241 Full Color Softcover $45.00

FORTY GOSPEL GREATS FOR BANJO
by Eddie Collins

When you hear the term "Gospel Banjo," many assume we are talking about tunes you hear at every bluegrass festival-tunes in the Southern Gospel tradition. While these definitely make for good banjo fare, Eddie sought to cover new ground, of the 40 popular songs included, nearly 20 of them have not been previously arranged for banjo, plus lyrics have been placed below each melody note to give the player a sense of when to stress notes in order to bring out the melody above the fill-notes of the rolls. Each song is played on the enclosed CD. These 40 Gospel Greats for Banjo are both enjoyable and inspirational.
00001497 Book/CD Pack..$19.99

CELTIC SONGS FOR THE TENOR BANJO
37 Traditional Songs and Instrumentals
by Dick Sheridan

Jigs & reels, hornpipes, airs, dances and more are showcased in this exciting 37 collection drawn from Ireland, Scotland, Wales, Cornwall, Brittany and the Isle of Man. Each traditional song – with its lilting melody and rich accompaniment harmony – has been carefully selected and presented for tenor banjo in both note form and tablature with chord symbols and diagrams. Lyrics and extra verses are included for many songs. Includes: All Through The Night, Blackbird Will You Go, The Campbells Are Coming, Garry Owen, Harvest Home, O'Gallaher's Frolics, Saddle The Pony, Swallow Tail Jig and many more.
00122477..$14.99

OLD TIME STRING BAND BANJO STYLES
by Joseph Weidlich

POld Time String Band Banjo Styles will introduce you to the traditional, rural string band banjo styles as played in the southern mountains of the eastern United States, which were used to "second" vocal songs and fiddle tunes during the Golden Age of recorded string band music, from the early 1920s through the early 1930s. Includes: Historical Background , String Band Transcriptions of Selected Backups and Solos, Building a Thumb-lead Style Backup.
00123693..$19.99

TRAD JAZZ FOR TENOR BANJO

by Dick Sheridan

Part of a universal repertoire familiar to all traditional jazz musicians, the 35 standards in this collection are arranged for the tenor banjo but chord symbols make playing suitable for all banjo tunings as well as other chord instruments. Popular keys have been chosen, with melodies in notes and tab, plus large, easy-to-read chord diagrams, lyrics, commentary and more. Includes: Margie, Wabash Blues, Tishmigo Blues, Avalon, Shine, Back Home Again in Indiana, Shinny like My Sister Kate, St. Louis Blues, Jazz Me Blues, Old Green River, By and By, Yellow Dog Blues and more.
00139419 Book/CD Pack..$19.99

BOB CARLIN - FIDDLE TUNES FOR CLAWHAMMER BANJO
by Bob Carlin

Renowned instructor and Grammy nominee Bob Carlin is one of the best-known banjoists performing today. This book, an update of his 1983 classic with the welcome addition of a CD, teaches readers how to play 32 best-loved pieces from his first two solo recordings: Fiddle Tunes for Clawhammer Banjo and Where Did You Get That Hat? Includes fantastic photos from throughout Bob's career.
00001327 Book/CD Pack..$19.99

GOSPEL BANJO
arranged by Dennis Caplinger

Features 15 spiritual favorites, each arranged in 2 different keys for banjo. Includes: Amazing Grace, Crying Holy, I'll Fly Away, In the Sweet By and By, Just a Closer Walk with Thee, Life's Railway to Heaven, Nearer My God to Thee, Old Time Religion, Swing Low, Sweet Chariot, Wayfaring Stranger, Will the Circle Be Unbroken, more!
00000249..$12.95

5 STRING BANJO NATURAL STYLE
No Preservatives
by Ron Middlebrook

Now available with a helpful play-along CD, this great songbook for 5-string banjo pickers features 10 easy, 10 intermediate and 10 difficult arrangements of the most popular bluegrass banjo songs. This book/CD pack comes complete with a chord chart.
00000284..$17.95

P.O. Box 17878 - Anaheim Hills, CA 92817

(714) 779-9390   www.centerstream-usa.com

NEW FROM CENTERSTREAM

You'll Like What You Hear

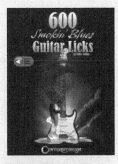

600 SMOKIN BLUES GUITAR LICKS
by Eddie Collins
00361243......................... $19.99

500 SMOKIN COUNTRY GUITAR LICKS
by Eddie Collins
00327835......................... $19.99

ASAP BEGINNING BLUEGRASS BANJO
by Ron Middlebrook with Dick Sheridan
00295683......................... $14.99

TIN PAN ALLEY FAVORITES FOR FINGERSTYLE GUITAR
by Glenn Wieser
00356645......................... $19.99

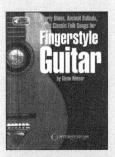

EARLY BLUES, ANCIENT BALLADS AND CLASSIC FOLK SONGS FOR FINGERSTYLE GUITAR
by Glenn Wieser
00323564......................... $14.99

RICHIE VALENS: HIS GUITARS AND MUSIC
by Ryan Sheeler
00292570......................... $19.99

SAD SONGS OF SORROW & MOURNING FOR THE UKULELE
by Dick Sheridan
00350526......................... $17.99

ASAP BEGINNING 4-STRING BASS METHOD
by Brian Emmel
00319871......................... $12.99

ULTIMATE COLLECTION OF WALTZES & OTHER SONGS IN 3/4 TIME FOR THE UKULELE
by Dick Sheridan
00302018......................... $19.99

5-STRING BANJO SET-UP & MAINTENANCE
by Todd Taylor
00346349......................... $29.99

ASAP TRUMPET FINGERING CHART
by Gerald F. Knipfel
00337782......................... $3.49

GUITAR DREAMS
by Andy Volk
00390187......................... $19.95

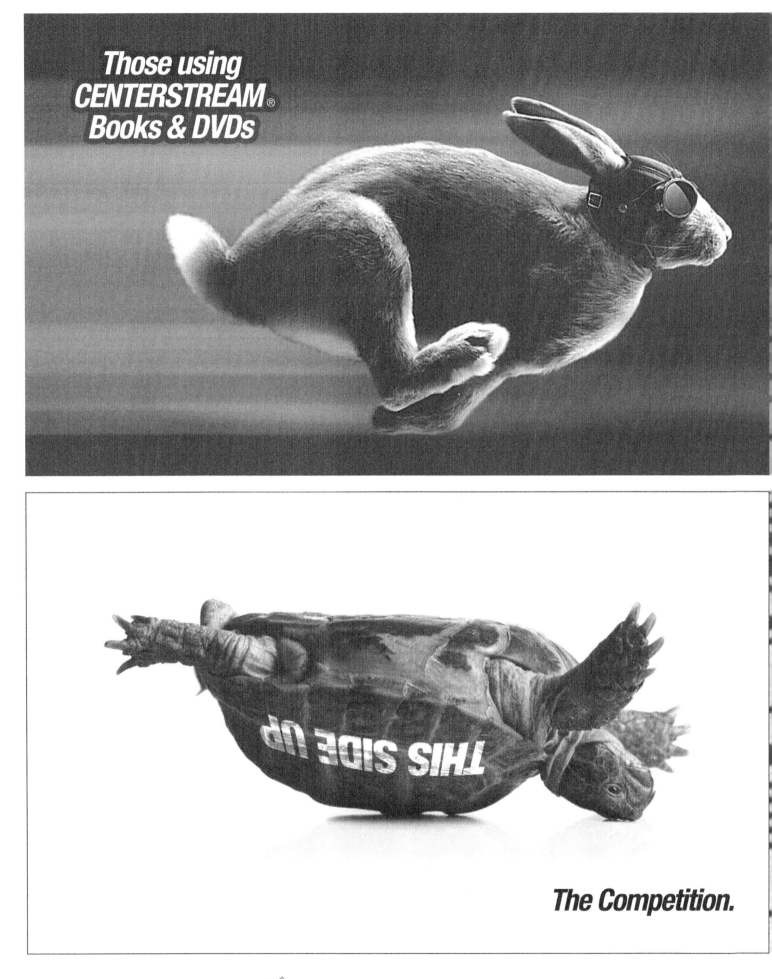